Conley Bottom

A Poemoir

Benjamin B. White

Conley Bottom
A Poemoir

Note: A "poemoir" is half poem, half memoir
Cover Art: Photo courtesy of Conley Bottom Resort

By the same author:

The Recon Trilogy +1
Running Wild Press
November 2020

Conley Bottom Boat Dock (circa 1970)

(Original Art courtesy of Rebecca Martin)

Born and raised eight miles from Conley Bottom, Ben White is a native of Monticello, Kentucky. However, he has taken his 22 years of military service (US Army & US Coast Guard), an associates, two bachelors, three masters, and a doctorate to settle in the enchanted lands of New Mexico.

Ben is the author of a book-length poem, *The Buddha Bastinado Blues*, an e-novel of the Cold War, *The Kill Gene*, and a novella-in-poem-form (a *poevella*), *The Cuban*. His poems have appeared in the anthologies *Incoming: Sex, Drugs, and Copenhagen*, and *Proud To Be: Writing by American Warriors*, volumes 6 and 7. He has also had work - poems, short stories, and non-fiction essays - appear in the Exterminating Angel Press Magazine, The Purple Breakfast Review, Akashic Books Online, Tuck Magazine, and The Sea Letter.

You can usually find him starting to write everyday around 4AM, and in his spare time, he teaches Business Administration classes for the Central New Mexico Community College, Human Resource Management classes for the University of Maryland Global Campus, and English classes for the Southwestern Indian Polytechnic Institute. He's also been known to edit anthologies and novels for Running Wild Press.

Conley Bottom
-1-

Summer had a taste
For bologna
And cheese sandwiches
With tomatoes
And Tom's plain potato chips
At the lake
With a towel spread out
On the rocks
At Conley Bottom,

But summer
Gives way
To autumn,
And flavor
Is just another memory.

Conley Bottom
      -2-

At any given time
You would see
Any given person
Because Conley Bottom
Was a good place to go
When you needed
A good place to go,

                   So,
Billy Boils and I
Happened to be there
At the same time one day
And like the second-grade
Best friends we were
                    We entertained ourselves
Throwing rocks at a log.

Ten years later,
Billy was dead
With a bullet
In his own head,
                    But I've always held
him
In the arms of my memory
Throwing rocks
At Conley Bottom.

Conley Bottom
-3-

A single mother at the lake
Wearing a two-piece bathing suit
Was the flame
For moth-like men
Who would try to impress her
By entertaining her children.

                              I always thought
Their stories,
And tricks,
And the ability
To pry off the cap
Of a Coke bottle
                              With their teeth
Were all about me

                              Because
My innocence
Was raised to be
                              Naïve.

Conley Bottom
-4-

                    The Monkees,
The Young Rascals,
The Turtles,
And Tommy James
                    Were always on the
stereo,
And singing me
An understanding
Of life,
                    So one day
I saw my older brother
Walking along the lake
At Conley Bottom
                    Arm-in-arm
                    With Sue Boston,
And I knew
He was just groovin'
On a Sunday afternoon.

Conley Bottom
-5-

In 1966,
My family came back
From Alaska broken
                With parents
divorced
And tension spoken
In the actions
Of friends and neighbors
Unable to welcome
                The pieces back
together,
But childhood
Was meant to weather
The storms of the older
                Generations,
So I was protected
From the missing relationships,
The juggling of money,
And the closing
                Of communities

As I was allowed to float
And experience
The tranquility
                Of Conley Bottom.

Conley Bottom
-6-

They meant to have
The farms, and barns,
And fences bulldozed down and out
                    Of the bottom land
With communities, country stores,
Churches, and cemeteries
                    Cleared before
The dam backed up the Cumberland
With rising waters
Flooding the lives
And home sites
                    Of the displaced,

But they didn't meet the deadline,
And the lake was haunted
By history drowning.

Conley Bottom
-7-

Memorial Day
Filled up the campgrounds
With Buckeyes from Ohio
Who had to bring their own beer
On their dry-county holidays,
                And who behaved in a way
That expected locals to bow down
And serve their every need
As they skied and swam,
Boating and fishing from the dam
All the way back to Somerset
                        Caught in the net
Of bait shops and convenient stores
That were forced to ignore
Their up-north attitudes
                        For the sake of sales
As they paid double-the-price
For ice, charcoal, sunscreen,
Bread, and Cokes
                        Never hearing the
jokes
We told about their excursions
With exaggerated perversions
                        To give them
character.

Aunt Gussie and I
Would fish from the bank
Up from the far side of the dock
Keeping any and every hook-full
We caught to clean, roll in corn meal,
And fry without worrying or caring
About the size or species,
                    But always ready
To compliment our angler skills
When she was too old,
And I was too young
To need a fishing license
                    To make what
                    We were doing
Anything more
Than Tom-Sawyer recreation,

And as soon as I turned 16,
And required state-issued
Permission to fish
                    I never cast another
line.

Conley Bottom
-9-

Eight miles from Monticello,
I was always on
The Wayne County side
                    Of the lake knowing
The bottom would drop off
Pretty quick, so staying
Close to the shore,
But still wondering,
                    If I should learn
                    How to swim,
Could I make it across
To get a view
From the Russell County side?

It was a deep and consistent
Sense of belonging
That kept that question
                    Unanswered.

Conley Bottom
-10-

I always maintained a mindset
That the first girl I loved
Would be the last girl I loved,
                    And there was
                    Karen Stinson
In my 1964 Chevrolet
With her nice, big

Green eyes

Full of her broader experience
And physical longing
As we were parked
At the top of the boat ramp
Not secluded enough to do more
Than talk, kiss, and watch the windows
Steam up with her growing frustration
                    With me
As I was lost and silly
In a spiders and snakes kind of way
Already regretting letting her
Forever get away –
                    As we were never
                    That close again.

Conley Bottom
-11-

In dry seasons –

                    Those years without
much rain –
The lake levels dropped,
And we could walk
Where we would normally swim,
                    And we'd find
Old rusty nails
That once held together
Barns and fences long gone,

                    And though we
loved
Having a lake, and we knew
The dam provided electricity,
We still had to wonder
                    About the lives
                    And livelihoods
Of those relocated people
Who had farms
And homes
                    Along the river.

Conley Bottom
-12-

My mechanic brother received
A 1960 Ford Falcon
From our musician brother
Who had received it
From our Plymouth-driving mother
Who had received it
                    After the divorce,
And it was a solid, well-kept car,
But if he had sold it as is,
It might have gotten 50 dollars,
                    So my mechanic
brother
Took the doors off
And camouflaged the Falcon
In a U. S. Army jungle pattern,
And sold it for 100 dollars
Because then it had adventurous
character
And Kentucky curb appeal –

                    And to this day,
Up on the hill from Conley Bottom
Among the Christmas tree pines,
There are the light-blue doors
Of a 1960 Ford Falcon
Mysteriously rusting away
Without explanation.

Conley Bottom
-13-

My mother would quack
At the ducks on the boat ramp,
And the mother duck
Would quack back –
                    And I am sure
The line of ducklings
Were just as embarrassed
As the line of children.

Conley Bottom
-14-

My Air Force brother
Had been discharged
And sent home from Vietnam
Swinging through Texas
To get his young wife,
And move her into the trailer
At Conley Bottom –

                    What had been
Someone's vacation trailer
Was now going to be
Their first home together,

But Wayne County, Kentucky
Was a long way from Austin, Texas,
And some adjustments
                    Don't come easy
No matter how much
Newlywed love
Can fill a double-wide.

Conley Bottom
-15-

We were just a handful
Of local boys
Hanging out
With the out-of-state campers
                    When one of us
Flipped a beer bottle
At the girl from Indiana
And chipped her tooth.

                    She was too drunk
To write down the address
He gave her,
But it didn't matter;
                    There was no such
                    Address anyway.

Conley Bottom
-16-

                          It was classless –
As a couple of us walked through
The campsite and stopped
To watch how people act
  When they are away from home
Unknown, unwatched, unjudged
                          And drunk –

A couple inside a tent
Had propped up a lantern
To cast their simulated
                          Sex-act silhouettes
On the canvas to get a crowd
Gathered laughing at the scene

                          While Conley
Bottom innocence
Was replaced by the decadence
Of tasteless recreation
Passed off
                          As vacation
entertainment.

Conley Bottom
-17-

It was a warm summer night –
                    And weren't they
all? –
With my brothers and sisters
And me all gathered
At the Conley Bottom trailer
When I first heard
                    Janis Joplin,
And I was a little too young
To appreciate
What Playboy Magazine
Had called her whisky fire voice,

                    But my oldest sister
With deep admiration
Told me
To respect the dead,
                    And at that moment
Tucked in the woods
Up the hill from the lake
                    I gave Janice
A piece of my heart.

Conley Bottom
-18-

After we had asked
If we could go to the lake
With our neighbor,
                Our mother said
yes,
So we headed
To Conley Bottom,
                But from the
highway
Across the neighborhood,
Looking back at our house,
We saw our mother
Standing on the carport
                        Waving a towel –

We figured
She was just waving goodbye.

                        We didn't know
When she agreed
For us to go
She had gone inside
                To change clothes
                And be included.

Conley Bottom
-19-

The day would spend its time
Sucking moisture up from the surface
Of the lake to build heat
Into a storm with clouds
                    Darkening the
distance
Above the horizon where the humidity
Would bend itself over,
Rising and folding; rising and folding,
Gaining energy with lightning
                    And thunder
Needing a place to go,
And we watched the weather
Holding its promise to break
The summer stagnation –

                    The wind chimes
Hanging in the archway
Between the kitchen and the living room
Gently moved
With a soft tinkle
Hinting of rain
                    Along the edge
Of a slight breeze
From eight miles away.

Miss Eva
Was always there
At the Conley Bottom Boat Dock
                  Like a barnacle
As she worked
Selling miscellaneous lake necessities,
Frying hamburgers,
And serving French fries –
                  And they were
The best fries in Wayne County
Slapped down on the counter
With salt, ketchup,
And her opinion,
                    So you could sit
On the stool
Enjoying a big platter
                    Full of potatoes,
And have your life
Straightened out
At the same time.

Conley Bottom
-21-

My first-sister-in-law,
Who had probably had enough
Of Conley Bottom, Wayne County,
Monticello, and Kentucky altogether,
                    Was on the verge of
divorce,
                    And headed back to
Texas
When she pretty much sealed the deal
By attacking my brother
With a butcher knife
While he was working
                    At the boat dock.

                    Her intent –
evidently –
Was to take an everlasting stab
At the future of their marriage
In a *Play Misty for Me*
                    Kind of way.

                    My brother always
          said,
                    He just took the
          knife
                    Away from her
                    The best he could.

Conley Bottom
-22-

Tynt Upchurch
Only had a few fingers left
After he plugged a corn mill
That was leaking ground up corn –
                    It would have been
safer
                    To have turned it off
first –
And he lived in a trailer
A little ways up from the lake
Until he watched it get blown
Over the bluff by a tornado
One night in 1974
As he sat in his red Dodge thankful
He'd decided to take his chances
                    In his car –

The next day, he went over the hill
To see what could be salvaged,
And he saw with his own eyes
A forty-pound gopher
That the storm had sucked up
                    Into a Coke bottle.
That story never changed –
Though he always told
Anyone listening
It was up to them
                    To believe it or not.

It takes characters
To give a place character.

Conley Bottom
-23-

The Vietnam veterans
Working together at the boat dock
Pumping gas for the tourists
Would get off work at midnight,
                          And then
Still wearing their fatigues
They'd take off their jungle boots,
And strap on skies
To daredevil across the black-water
Surface of the lake
                          Without any regard
                          For the unseen
dangers
Of dead-head logs
And driftwood,

But if the danger hadn't been there,
They still would not have gone straight
home –
                          They would have
had
To find
The discharged adrenaline thrill
                          Somewhere else.

Conley Bottom
-24-

The autumn lake is quiet
With a chill hovering
Over its summer echoes
And the ghosts
                    Of forgotten
moments
Sitting on the shore
With knees tucked
To their chins
                    Trying to pretend
They can escape
The life-defying events
That might as well
                    Never have
happened
If history
Was going to let them go
                    Anyway.

Conley Bottom
-25-

At one time,
I might have walked through
The parked trucks
                    With their empty
trailers,
And wished I, too,
Had a boat,
Or at least could have been able
To launch
                    And get underway
With someone who did –

                    But after a while,
I matured to the point
Of being able to sit
In the sun beside the lake,
                    And be satisfied
With what I did
And didn't have.

Conley Bottom
-26-

I was 10 or 11 years old
When my Air Force brother came home
And moved into the trailer
                    At Conley Bottom
Where he was quiet and distant,
And maybe not quite all the way home
yet,
With his GI fatigues,
His jungle boots cut into sandals,
His Yosemite Sam Gunfighters
                    Of Da Nang plaque,
And a giant wooden Buddha
                    With dog tags
hanging
                    Around its neck,

And even the fear I had
                    Of my brother
                    Idolized him
While the musty smell of the trailer,
The gasoline smell of the boat dock,
The fresh water smell of the lake,
The earthy smell of the dirt and trees,
And the constant smell of heat and
humidity
                    All saturated my
curiosity
With an obsession
That equated that scene
                    And scenery
                    With Vietnam.

Conley Bottom
-27-

The Fury would fill up
With a backseat full of children,
And a trunk full of excitement
Holding blow-up floaties and rafts
                    With a summertime
smell
                    Of new plastic
From the Dollar General Store
Waiting for huffs and puffs
To press against
The stiff and stuck shapes
That filled up with air
                    Two lungs full at a
time
Until the teeth clamped down
On the plastic valve
With a tongue ready
To maneuver the plug
Over and in to hold the inflated fun
                    In place
To splash into the lake
Where we'd spend the day
The way summer
                    Was meant
                    To be spent.

Conley Bottom
-28-

Nothing said Conley Bottom
Like Styrofoam

                              From the cheap
body boards
                              We got at Rose's
Department Store
                              To float around on
                              And propel with
strokes and kicks,

To the white cooler
Full of squeaky picnic –
Ice, cheese, bologna,
Bread, and cold drinks,

                              To the small
molecules,
                              Chunks, and pieces
                              Discarded and
floating in
                              On the waves in the
wake
                              Of houseboats,

As convenience
Was cheap, and disposable,
And fun while it lasted.

Conley Bottom
-29-

The security lights of lakefront cabins
Over on the Russell County side
Would shine and float
Skimming along the surface
                              Of the lake
Competing with the moon
For warm attention and comfort
Seeping into the description
Of beauty
                              Balanced between
The waves of light
And the waves of water.

Conley Bottom
-30-

It was cheap recreation –
                    A day at the lake –
And we were in need
Of low-cost activities
To get us out of the house
And away from the reminders
Of broken-family socio-economics,
                    And it was special
To swim and splash the day away,
And sometimes you could find
A warmer column of water
Holding heat like a hidden
                    Hot tub below the
surface
And it would suspend us
In feelings of escape –

                    Escape
From the heat and humidity,
But also
From the growing attitudes
Of exclusion we were feeling
From the community
In which we belonged,
                    But weren't
welcome.

Conley Bottom
-31-

On the Federal land
Up on the Conley Bottom hill,
There was a stand
Of pine trees,
                          And every
Christmas
Was celebrated
With a government contribution,
Machete-hacked and brought back,
To decorate
With an appreciation
Of the freedom
To enjoy it.

Conley Bottom
-32-

My grown and settled brother
Had a house and barn
On six acres at Conley Bottom,
But the mosaics of hard times
Set a pattern, and it was all
                    Auctioned off –
The house,
The barn,
The acres,
The cars,
The equipment,
                    Sold off
To shut down
And sever the connection
To that part
Of the county.

Conley Bottom
-33-

It had been a boat dock,
A boat ramp, a swimming beach,
Some vacation trailers,
And a campground –
                    That was Conley
Bottom –
Just a place
Where Wayne County
Touched the manmade lake,
So boats could launch or refuel,
And families could swim and picnic
                    Or walk the shores
                    On a Sunday
evening,
But it wasn't good enough,
Not appealing enough,
Not rich enough
                    To leave well-
enough alone.
So Conley Bottom
Had to be transformed
Into a resort –

                    Conley Bottom
Resort –

While its history full of stories
Was lost under the polish
Of marketed profits...

                    But some places
have roots
That run deeper
Than any tourist
Would even care
To uncover.

Conley Bottom
-34-

A '64 Impala
            Two-door hardtop
            283
Three-on-the-tree –

Classic –

With sportability
Hugging highways
Back from the lake
To the house for supper
Or into Monticello
To play softball
At the park –

Cruising –

Heat and humidity
Swirling and chilling
The sweat soaking
And sticking
            A t-shirt
            To the front seat
Taking the two-lane curves
At sixty
Without a care or concern –
            Just a summer to burn
Never considering
Anything would change
Until it all did
            Turning those drives
To and from Conley Bottom
Into just a thought,
A memory, a dream,
A poem...

But a poem written
With the windows rolled down.

www.ingramcontent.com/pod-product-compliance
Lightning Source LLC
Chambersburg PA
CBHW021130070726
47591CB00014B/2225